![Collins]

easy learning

Reading and rhyme bumper book

Ages 3–5

cat   hat

bat

Carol Medcalf

How to use this book

- Find a quiet, comfortable place to work, away from distractions.

- This book has been written in a logical order, so start at the first page and work your way through.

- Help with reading the instructions where necessary and ensure that your child understands what to do.

- Help your child sound out the rhyming sounds as you work through the book together. This will help them to hear the rhymes more clearly. Try to share many more rhymes and stories with your child to complement the activities in this book.

- All children learn and develop at a different rate. If an activity is too difficult for your child, then do more of our suggested practical activities (see Parent's tips) and return to the page when you know that they are likely to achieve it.

- Always end each activity before your child gets tired so that they will be eager to return next time.

- Help and encourage your child to check their own answers as they complete each activity.

- Let your child return to their favourite pages once they have been completed. Talk about the activities they enjoyed and what they have learned.

Special features of this book:

- **Parent's tip:** situated on every left-hand page, this suggests further activities and encourages discussion about what your child has learned.

- **Progress panel:** situated at the bottom of every right-hand page, the number of stars shows your child how far they have progressed through the book. Once they have completed each double page, ask them to colour in the blank star.

- **Certificate:** the certificate on the last page should be used to reward your child for their effort and achievement. Remember to give your child plenty of praise and encouragement, regardless of how they do.

Published by Collins
An imprint of HarperCollins*Publishers* Ltd
The News Building
1 London Bridge Street
London
SE1 9GF

Browse the complete Collins catalogue at www.collins.co.uk

© HarperCollins*Publishers* Ltd 2018

10 9 8 7 6 5 4

ISBN 9780008275440

The author asserts the moral right to be identified as the author of this work.

All rights reserved. No part of this publication may be reproduced, stored in a retrieval system, or transmitted, in any form or by any means, electronic, mechanical, photocopying, recording or otherwise, without the prior permission of Collins.

British Library Cataloguing in Publication Data

A Catalogue record for this publication is available from the British Library

All images and illustrations are
© shutterstock.com and
© HarperCollins*Publishers*

Author: Carol Medcalf
Commissioning Editor: Michelle I'Anson
Project Manager: Rebecca Skinner
Cover Design: Sarah Duxbury
Text Design and Layout: QBS Learning
Illustration: Jenny Tulip
Production: Natalia Rebow
Printed in Great Britain by Martins the Printers

Contents

What can you see?

- Talk about all the things in the picture. What can you see?

Odd one out

Circle the odd one out in each row.

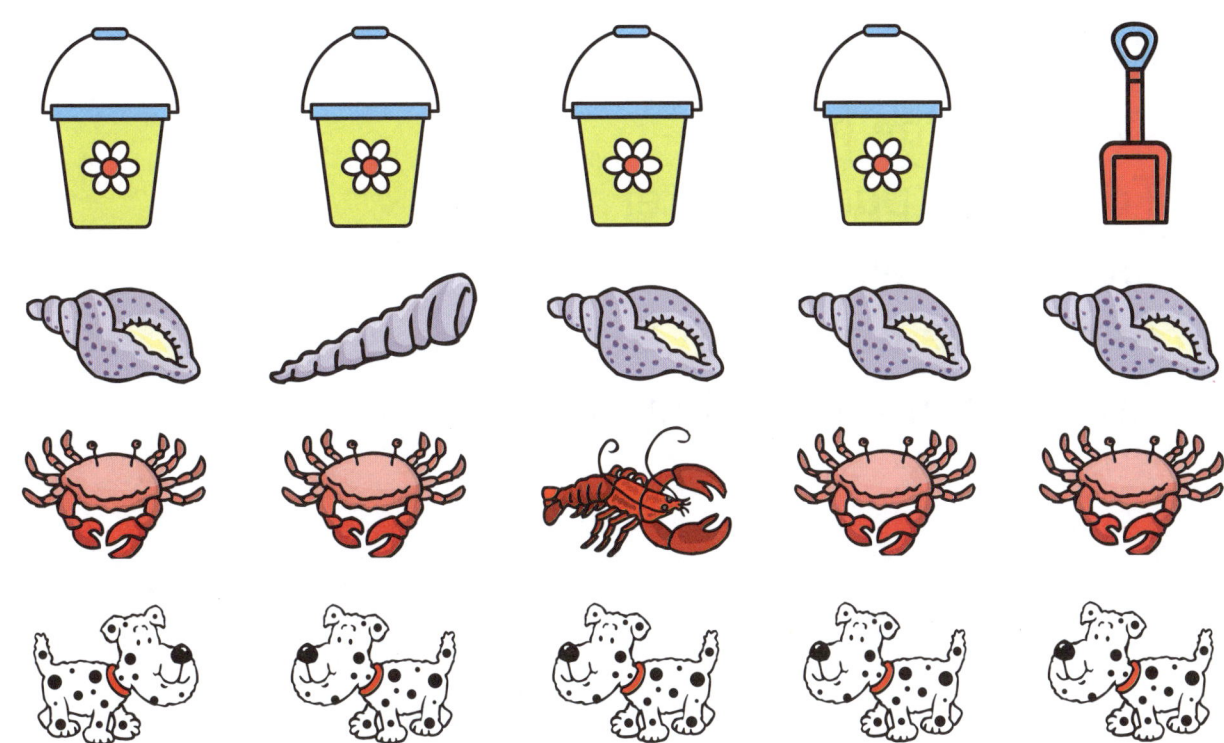

Draw a flag  on the sandcastle that is different from the others.

Well done! Now colour the star.

Rhymes

● Trace and colour the picture of Jack and Jill.

Jack and Jill
Went up the hill,
To fetch a pail of water.
Jack fell down
And broke his crown,
And Jill came tumbling after.

More rhymes

- Say the rhyme and colour the picture.

  Incy Wincy Spider climbed up the water spout.
  Down came the rain and washed poor Incy out.
  Out came the sunshine and dried up all the rain,
  So Incy Wincy Spider climbed up the spout again.

Well done!
Now colour
the star.

Spot the difference: pictures

● There are **five** differences between the two pictures. Draw a circle around each difference.

Many letters and words look very similar. By developing their observational skills, it will be easier for your child to spot these differences.

Spot the difference: words

- <u>Underline</u> the differences in each pair of words.

boat   goat

bear   pear

- Cross (✗) the word that is different in each row.

ball   ball   wall   ball

box   fox   fox   fox

light   light   light   night

Story time: *Jess* (part 1)

● Look at these four pictures.
  Say what you think is happening to tell the story.

1.

2.

Before children are given books with words to read, they start by telling a story through looking at pictures.
Let your child tell the story as they see it. You can then say what you think the story is about.

3.

4.

Well done!
Now colour
the star.

Middle a sound

- Draw a line to match each word to the correct picture.

cat

bag

tap

hat

bat

- Say each word. If the word has an **a** sound in the middle that you can see and hear, colour the apple green.

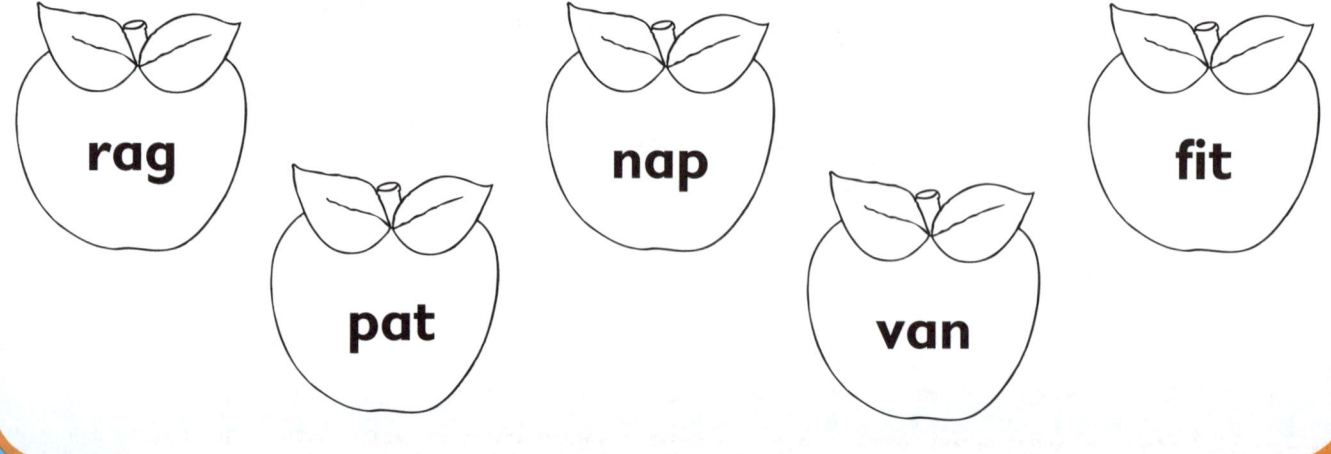

rag

pat

nap

van

fit

CVC (consonant, vowel, consonant) words are the best place to start reading. They are generally phonetic, so they can be sounded out, i.e. the word can be heard by saying the individual letters quickly, such as c-a-t, cat.

Middle e sound

- Circle the word that matches the picture at the start of each row.

   bed   cup   tap   ten

   tin   peg   cap   lad

   van   web   hot   pip

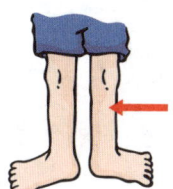   mix   bin   leg   sun

   bob   dig   bus   red

10   ten   top   wig   fed

Well done!
Now colour
the star.

Middle i sound

● Write the **i** sound in the middle of each word.
Read the word.

b_i_g   l_d

m__x   h__m

● Sound out each word.
Circle the word if you can hear an **i** sound in
the middle.

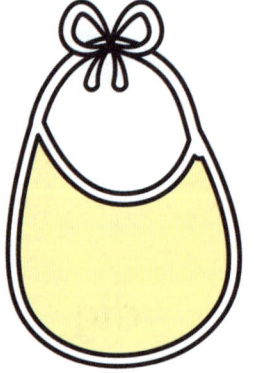

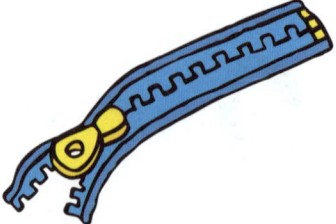

Middle o sound

● Say each word.
Trace the circle if you can hear an **o** sound in the middle.

  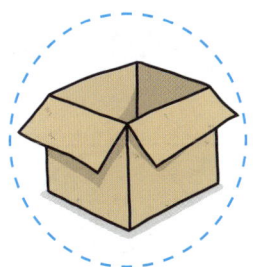

● Write the letter **o** in the middle of each word.
Read the word.

f_g   g_t   h_t

Well done!
Now colour
the star.

Middle u sound

- Trace each word.
  Circle the **u** sound in the word.

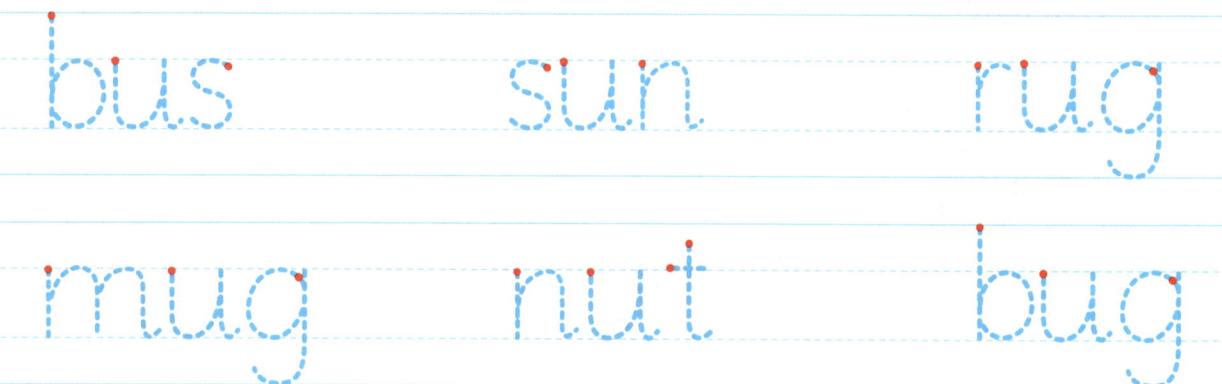

- Write the correct word under each picture.
  Copy the words from above.

___ ___ ___   ___ ___ ___

___ ___ ___   ___ ___ ___

CVC words

- Read each word.
  Find the item in the picture and circle it.

hat	cat	van	bag
bin	fox	dog	bus

Well done!
Now colour
the star.

Story time: *Jess* (part 2)

● Look at each picture.
Tell the story using the words to help you.

1.

Jess

2.

bed

First, sound the words out together by reading J-e-ss, b-e-d, s-i-t, b-all. Then look at the story again and ask your child what they think is happening.

3.

sit

4.

ball

Well done!
Now colour
the star.

19

Find the letter

● Which letter is missing from each word?
Write the letter to complete the word.

___un

___ed

___ug

___an

___ip

___en

___ap

___op

Nonsense words

- Read each word.
  Colour each boat that has a real word on it.
  Cross out (**X**) each boat that has a nonsense word on it.

pon

lip

mip

pet

den

hot

rof

Well done!
Now colour
the star.

At the park

Draw a line to match each word to part of the picture.

 bin

 sit

 fun

 run

 dog

 sun

Asking your child to match words to pictures is a great way to make sure they understand the meaning of the words. In the picture above, there is more than one possible option for words like 'sit' and 'fun'. Talk to your child about why they chose the one they did.

Colour and read

- Colour each picture and match it to the correct word.

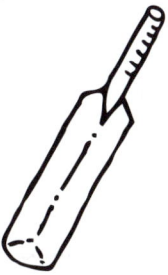

bat

doll

ted

cup

ship

- Read the colour.
  Use that colour to finish the pictures.

red

Well done!
Now colour
the star.

Sequence the story

● Write the numbers **1**, **2**, **3** and **4** in the boxes to put the pictures in order.

Don't worry if your child cannot read the words on the next page – it is a matching exercise. However, the colours are phonetic and can be read if your child is able to.

Word match

● Draw a line to match the word on each flag to the matching word on a lorry.

Well done!
Now colour
the star.

25

Rhyming words

● Draw a line to join the two words that rhyme in each row.

Talk about these rhyming words with your child. Point out that words that rhyme have the same sound at the end. Discuss different rhyming sounds and try to think of some rhyming words of your own.

Letter search

- Look at the picture at the start of each row.
  Colour the correct letters to make the word.

j a m p

k s u n

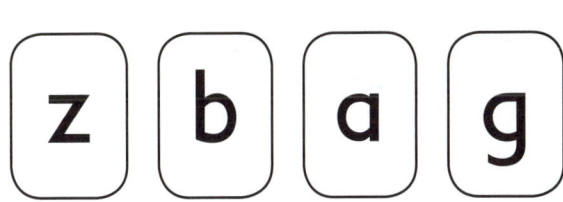

z b a g

b i b j

c w o t

Detective

- Find the words hidden in the picture and colour them in. Be careful – not all of them are real words!

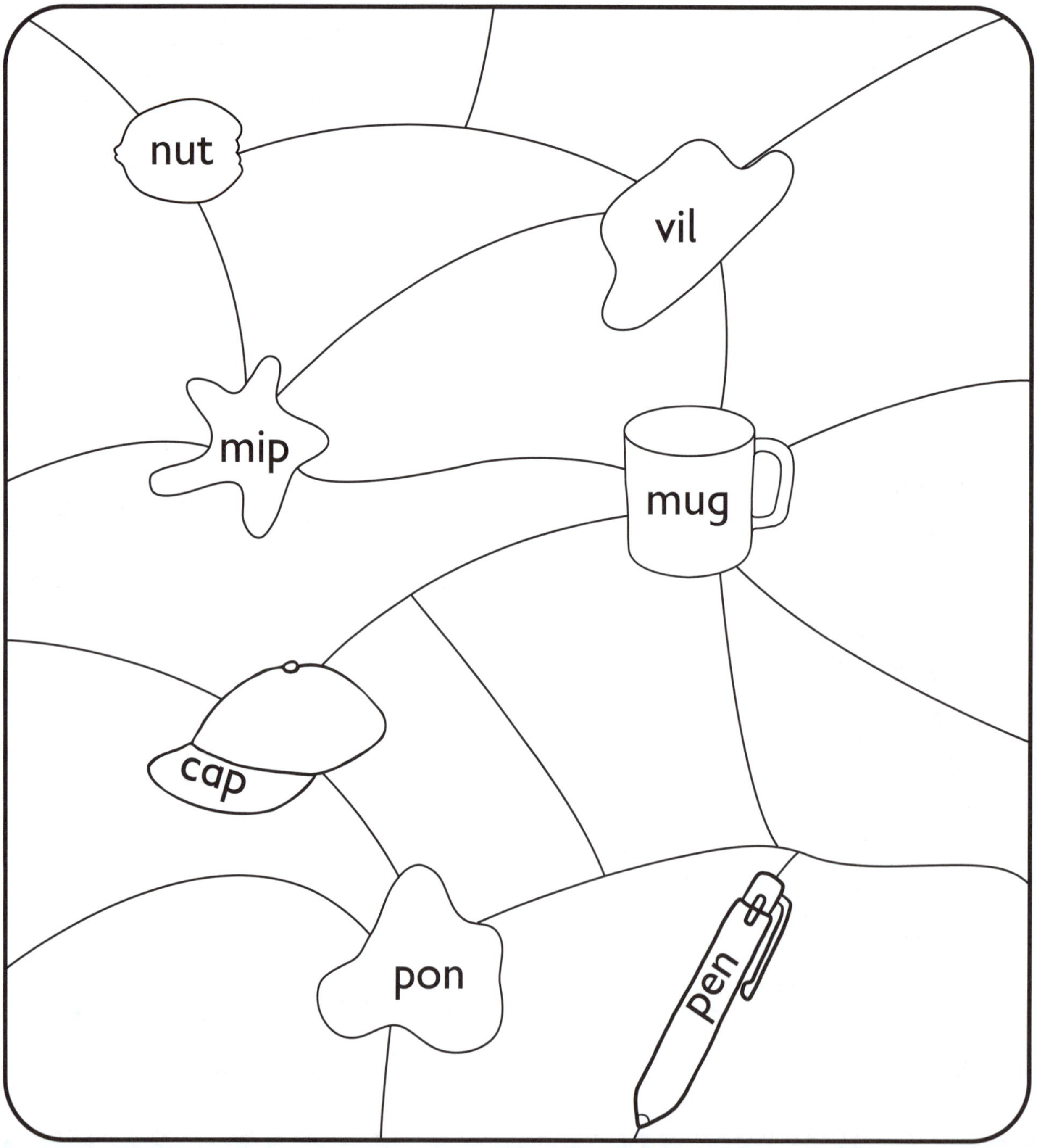

nut
vil
mip
mug
cap
pon
pen

Reading nonsense words aids reading skills as children can decode the word and know it is not a real word. Being able to do this aids self-correction when your child is older.

Spot the difference

● Look at the two pictures and circle 10 differences.

Well done!
Now colour
the star.

Tricky words

- Read these tricky words together.
  Learn to recognise them on your own.

  no   go   I   the   to   he   she

- Read these sentences using the tricky words above
  and phonetic sounds you know.

he is big

she is big

I go to the zoo

no I am not

High frequency words

- Read these tricky words together.
  Learn to recognise them on your own.
  Use coloured pens to trace over the sound lines and buttons.

— red   • blue

is   it   in   at   and

will   with   that   this

then   them   see   for

now   down   look   too

Well done!
Now colour
the star.

● Read the story.

Jess is sick

"Jess!"

"Jess is sick."

Help your child read each word by sounding out the letters, J-e-ss, i-s, s-i-ck, g-o, t-o, th-e, v-e-t, g-oo-d.

"Jess, go to the vet."

"Good Jess!"

Well done!
Now colour
the star.

Rhyme time

Choose and write the correct letter to start each word. Read all the rhyming words.

c h m b r

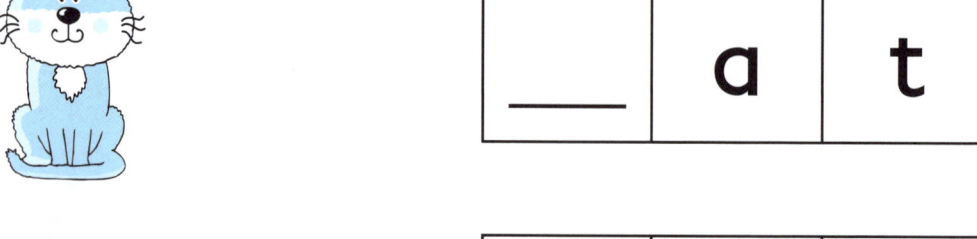

___ a t

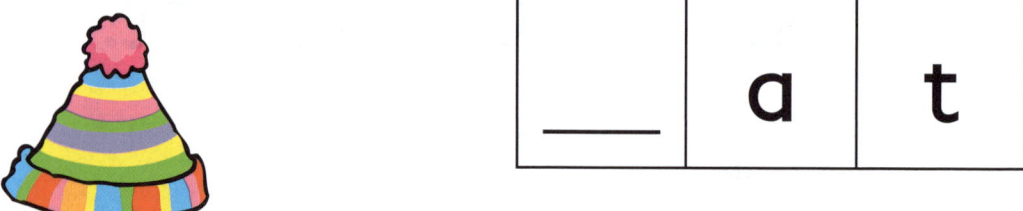

___ a t

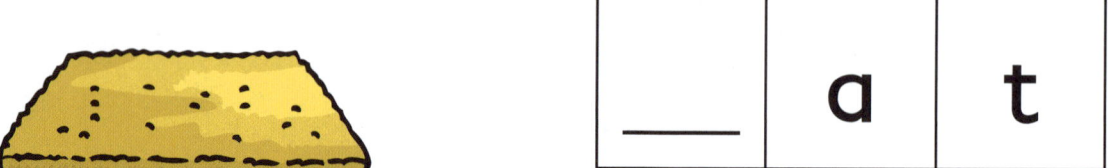

___ a t

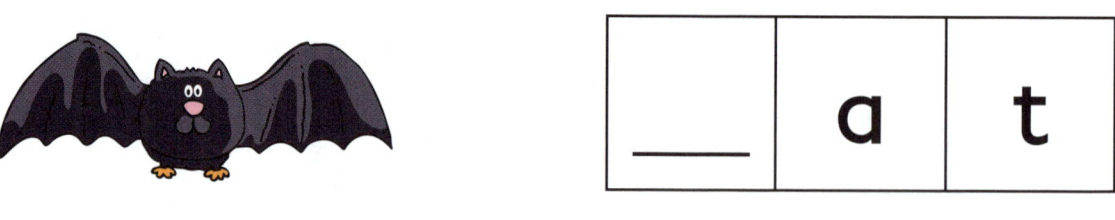

___ a t

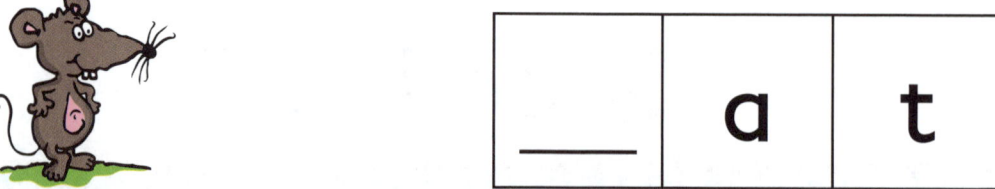

___ a t

Children often like playing rhyming games with their own name. Even if a real word does not rhyme, you can make up a word, e.g. 'Owen, bowen,' 'Holly, bolly,' 'Ruby, duby.'

Draw the story

● Read each rhyming sentence and draw a picture to match.

dog on a log

ball on a wall

More tricky words

● Read together and learn these words.

we

me

be

was

my

you

they

her

all

are

Again, use the sound lines and buttons to help with reading the words. If your child is not sure of the sounds that always go together, then more work on phonics using books and fun activities will help.

Wordsearch

The words below are hidden in the grid. Find the words and colour them.

big   hen   yes

mum   dad   box

m	u	m	x
z	d	a	d
b	i	g	o
j	h	e	n
y	e	s	l
b	o	x	q

Well done! Now colour the star.

Find the words

● Draw a line from each picture to the correct word. Colour each picture.

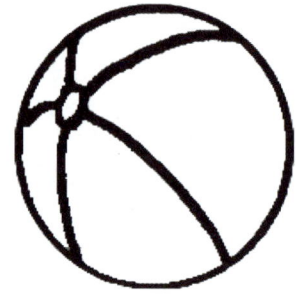

fish

ball

boat

car

drum

These words should be decoded by reading: f-i-sh, dr-u-m, b-all, c-ar, b-oa-t.

38

Which word?

● Read the two words in each box.
  Circle the word that matches the picture.

 bat bad	 dog din	 bin bee
 mug man	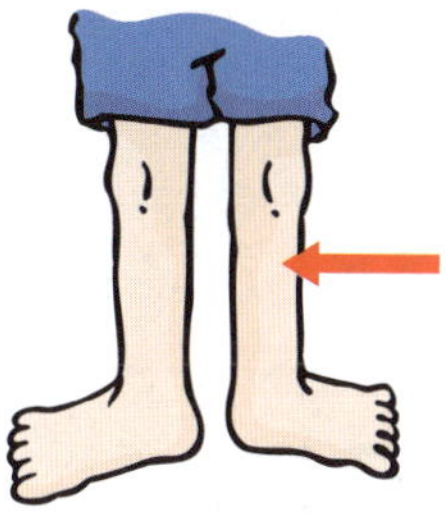 lot leg	 ball box
 rat ring	 fork fin	 doll duck

Well done!
Now colour
the star.

39

Find the word

● Look at the picture at the start of the row.
Find the word and draw a circle around it.

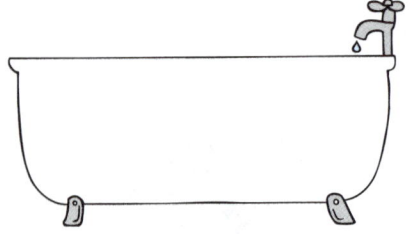

bath   then   that

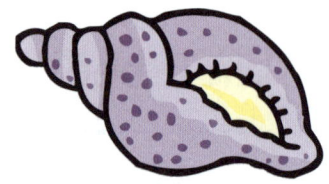

ship   shell   shop

room   zoom   book

moon   wood   mood

frog   food   roof

As children decode words again and again, such as c-a-p or m-u-g, they will eventually learn the word and will read it without having to separate each individual sound.

Odd one out: rhyming

- One word in each row does not rhyme with the others. Find the word that does not rhyme and cross (X) it out.

 jug

 mug

 slug

 plum

 fish

 cat

 mat

 rat

 frog

 log

 dog

 moon

 hat

 king

 sing

 ring

Well done! Now colour the star.

Story time: Jess (part 4)

● Read the story.

Jess is lost

"Jess."

"Did you see Jess?"
"No."

Help your child read each word by sounding out the letters. Here we have added a question mark. If your child has not come across one before, explain that this new symbol shows you are asking a question.

"Did you see Jess?"
"No."

"Jess!"

Well done!
Now colour
the star.

Answers

Page 4

Objects in picture to discuss include: children playing with a beach ball, someone under a beach umbrella, boats, crabs, shells, seagulls, sandcastle, bucket and spade.

Page 5

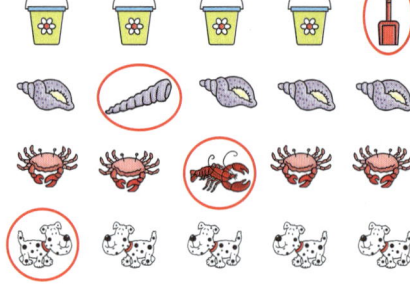

Page 6

Any colours can be used.

Page 7

Any colours can be used.

Page 8

Page 9

boat   **goat**

b<u>e</u>ar   **p<u>e</u>ar**

ball   ball   ~~wall~~   ball

~~box~~   fox   fox   fox

light   light   light   ~~night~~

Pages 10–11

Child's own story.

Page 12

cat
bag
tap
hat
bat

rag   nap   fit
pat   van

Page 13

 (bed) cup tap ten

tin (peg) cap lad

van (web) hot pip

mix bin (leg) sun

bob dig bus (red)

10 (ten) top wig fed

Answers

Page 14

b<u>i</u>g   l<u>i</u>d

m<u>i</u>x   h<u>i</u>m

6

Page 15

Any colours can be used.

f<u>o</u>g   g<u>o</u>t   h<u>o</u>t

Page 16

b<u>u</u>s   s<u>u</u>n   r<u>u</u>g

m<u>u</u>g   n<u>u</u>t   b<u>u</u>g

<u>s</u>un   <u>b</u>us

<u>m</u>ug   <u>n</u>ut

Page 17

Pages 18–19

Child's own story.

Page 20

<u>b</u>un

<u>r</u>ed

<u>m</u>ug

<u>f</u>an

<u>z</u>ip

<s>p</s>en

<u>c</u>ap

<u>m</u>op

Page 21

 <s>pon</s>

 lip

 <s>mip</s>

 pet

den

 hot

 <s>rof</s>

Page 22

Accept alternative answers for 'fun' and 'sit'.

bin   sit   fun

run   dog   sun

Page 23

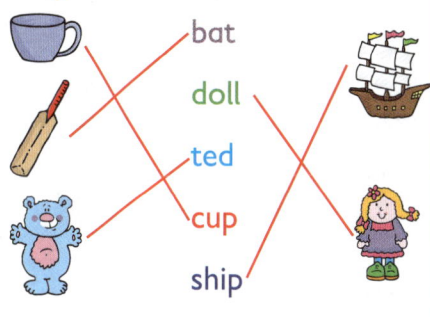

bat

doll

ted

cup

ship

Page 24

4

1

2

3

Answers

Page 25

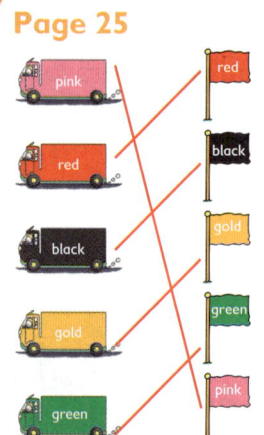

Page 26

Page 27

Any colours can be used.

 j a m p

 k s u n

 z b a g

 b i b j

 c w o t

Page 28

Any colours can be used.

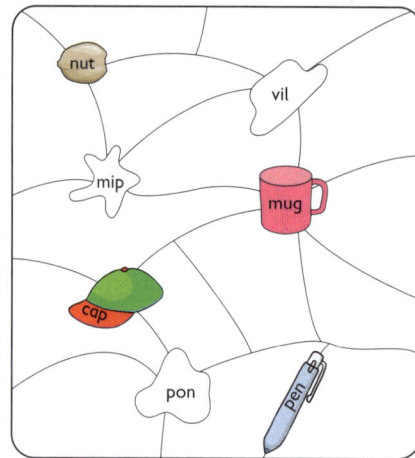

Page 29

Page 30

Read words with child. Repeat this exercise frequently.

Page 31

is   it   in   at   and

will   with   that   this

then   them   see   for

now   down   look   too

Pages 32–33

Child's own story.

Page 34

 | c | a | t |

 | h | a | t |

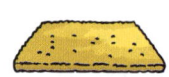 | m | a | t |

 | b | a | t |

 | r | a | t |

Page 35

Child's own drawings.

Page 36

Read words with child. Repeat this exercise frequently.

Page 37

Any colours can be used.

m	u	m	x
z	d	a	d
b	i	g	o
j	h	e	n
y	e	s	l
b	o	x	q

Answers

Page 38

Any colours can be used.

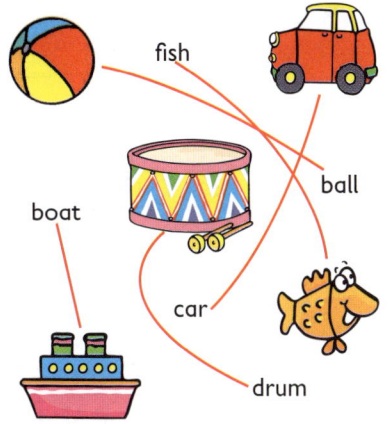

fish

car

boat

ball

drum

Page 39

(bat) bad	(dog) din	bin (bee)
(mug) man	lot (leg)	(ball) box
rat (ring)	(fork) fin	doll (duck)

Page 40

 (bath)   then   that

 ship   (shell)   shop

room   zoom   (book)

(moon)   wood   mood

(frog)   food   roof

Page 41

jug   mug   slug   ~~plum~~

~~fish~~   cat   mat   rat

frog   log   dog   ~~moon~~

~~hat~~   king   sing   ring

Pages 42–43

Child's own story.

Collins Easy Learning
Certificate of Achievement

Well Done!

This certificate is awarded to ....

for successfully completing ....

Date ....

Age ....

Signed ....

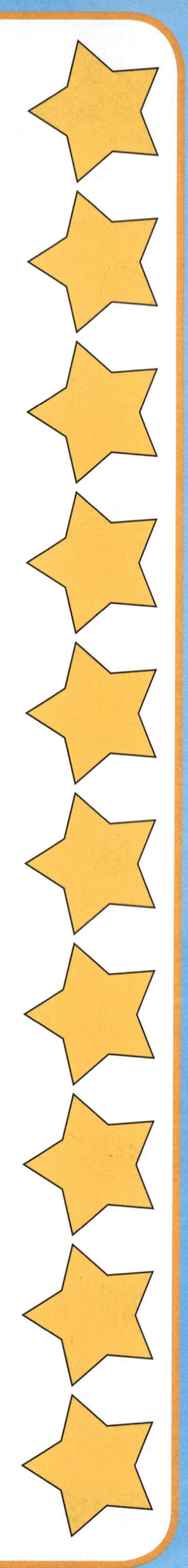